THE *PHEASANT*

BY
VIRGINIA C. HOLMGREN

EDITED BY
DR. HOWARD SCHROEDER

Professor in Reading and Language Arts
Dept. of Elementary Education
Mankato State University

PRODUCED AND DESIGNED BY
BAKER STREET PRODUCTIONS
Mankato, MN

CRESTWOOD HOUSE
Mankato, Minnesota

INTRODUCTION:

For ring-necked pheasants, March is the month when the new year begins. Birds that have been together in a winter flock scatter now. Each full-grown cock must find and claim the land that will be home for himself and his hens. It must be good land, with room for well-hidden nests and, someday, growing chicks.

To make his claim, a cock first finds a lookout post. It may be a rock, a log, a small rise of ground, a fence, or an old stone wall. It will be at least a little higher than the land around it so that he can see whatever there is to see. Now he mounts his post and lifts his head high. The white neck ring that gave him his name shows clearly against the darker feathers.

KOK! KOK! he calls in a voice that rings out like two bugle notes. He lifts his gold-flecked wings and claps them down against bronze-tone sides for a muffled double drum beat. Long tail plumes stream out like banners. No royal trumpeter sending out a challenge from atop a castle wall could make his meaning clearer: **This land is mine!** And somewhere near, brown-feathered hens are listening.

A cock pheasant claims his territory.

CHAPTER ONE:

The Asian homeland

The ring-neck's clear call is heard often now in the North American springtime. But there were no wild ring-necked pheasants — no wild pheasants of any kind — anywhere in the Americas until the 1880's. Asia is the pheasant homeland.

Ring-necks are native to China. Pheasants of other kinds are at home from northern China, Korea and Japan on southward and westward across Asia to the Black Sea. Some of them look very much like the Chinese ring-necks. Others are quite different in coloring. But all have long tail plumes. All are chicken-like in beak, body and behavior.

Pheasants come to Europe

The first Europeans to find pheasants were ancient Greek adventurers sailing to explore far Black Sea shores. They found these strange, long-

Some relatives of the ring-necked pheasant (left to right): silver, gold and Reeves.

tailed beauties beside the River Phasis, so they called them "Phasian birds." The Greeks took home as many as they could capture and then went back for more. In time, the Romans took both bird and word from the Greeks. The rest of Europe got both bird and word from the Romans. So the name sounds much the same in all European languages. In French it is **faisan.** In German and Swedish it is **fasan.** In Dutch it is **fazant.** And in English, of course, it is **pheasant.**

These Phasian birds were black-necked pheasants, without the white color. But ring-necks from China were also brought to Europe in later years. In most of Europe all pheasants were kept as half-tame birds on private estates. Only the wealthy landowner and his friends were allowed to shoot them or feast on their tender meat. Most common folk never got a close look. They knew that a pheasant was a big, brown, chicken-like bird. They knew it was supposed to be delicious eating. But that's all they knew about it.

Pheasants for North America

Most European colonists who came to America in the early days saw big brown birds in the woods and mistook them for pheasants. Usually these birds were ruffed grouse. Many people, however, went right on calling them pheasants even after they knew better.

Meanwhile, a few wealthy landowners in the East brought half-tame, black-necked pheasants from England. None of them ever lived more than a few months however.

In the autumn of 1880, a man named Owen Denny, a lawyer from Portland, Oregon, was sent to China to represent the United States as consul-general in the city of Shanghai. There Owen and his wife, Gertrude Jane, saw wild ring-necked pheasants in the fields and were delighted with their beauty. When the cook served roast pheasant for dinner, they were equally delighted with its delicious flavor. They made up their minds to send ring-necks back to Oregon. Owen and his wife knew that shipping the birds would be costly. But they believed that having such beautiful birds in Oregon would be worth the price.

A ruffed grouse that looks like a hen pheasant.

Owen and Gertrude Denny.

Early in 1881, they learned that a ship in Shanghai harbor would soon sail for Port Townsend, Washington. From there, the pheasants could easily be shipped to friends in Portland, Oregon, where they would be free to roam. So Denny arranged for some sixty birds, both cocks and hens, to be put into big covered baskets and sent by ship.

When the ship docked in Port Townsend in early March, 1881, most of the birds were alive and in good health. The moment they were off the ship, the birds caught sight of blue sky, earth and greenery. One look, and they were determined to get free. They struggled so hard to get out of the baskets that most of them battered themselves to death. Only seventeen pheasants were alive when they finally reached Portland.

These seventeen were set free on a farm on Sauvie Island, just outside Portland. It was a wild and lonely place. The pheasants might have been content there — except for one thing. Fourteen were cocks, and three were hens. Each pheasant cock is used to having at least two or three hens for himself. That's the way of the pheasant.

Now only two or three cocks could have a mate. The others all wandered off, looking for mates they would never find. Perhaps they were so troubled without a mate that they did not keep a sharp watch for enemies. At any rate, they all vanished.

Two of the three hens were seen with chicks during

the summer. Later, they seemed to vanish. If any were still alive by early winter, they kept well hidden.

Try, try again

Oregon friends wrote the Dennys that their birds had disappeared. Gertrude and Owen promptly decided to send more pheasants to Oregon. This time they found a ship sailing direct to Portland. They had a special cage put on board. It was huge — twenty feet high and twenty feet wide. The cage was set right out on deck where the birds would have good fresh air. Tubs of bamboo trees and other plants the pheasants knew were set round about. The floor of the cage was covered with sand and fine gravel. The pheasants could scratch in the sand or nibble the green leaves and feel right at home.

A few birds died, even with all this care. However, twenty-eight healthy pheasants arrived in Portland in March, 1882. There were ten cocks and eighteen hens. Every cock would have at least one mate and some would have two.

They were all set free on Peterson Butte, a wooded hill in Linn County near the Denny family homestead. Both friends and relatives living nearby promised to look out for these "China birds." And the China birds looked out for themselves. By mid-

Pheasants like a combination of trees, grass and shrubs. Luckily, Oregon had all three.

summer 1882, there were at least a dozen flocks of Oregon-born Chinese ring-necked pheasants.

Success at last

Oregon's pheasants had come to stay. No doubt of that. In 1884, the Dennys returned to the United

First hunting season

A cock pheasant busts out of a field.

Denny's story, and the pheasants themselves, really got around. In the ten years of protection, the pheasants from Peterson Butte spread out over an area one hundred eighty miles long and forty miles wide. And they made themselves right at home.

Sometimes a bold ring-neck cock would strut into a barnyard, challenge the rooster to a fight and win.

Then the ring-neck raider would get the hens together and drive them off to the woods. Needless to say, farm folk didn't like that. They could hardly wait for the ten years to be over so they could shoot every ring-neck in sight.

Ring-necks were clever at getting into gardens, too, and nibbling off tender shoots of lettuce or other green plants. Sometimes in summer a flock might get into a wheat field and have a feast for themselves before the farmer could harvest his crop.

Too many pheasants, everyone said. Hunters will take care of that!

And the hunters did. No count was kept, but some guessed that a good fifty thousand birds were taken in Oregon that first year. In 1893, over thirteen thousand birds were killed in Linn County alone, the county where the birds of 1882, had made that great start. Over thirteen thousand birds were killed and shipped to San Francisco markets. The pheasant story was no longer an Oregon secret.

Pheasants to share

From 1895 on, almost every state was writing to Oregon begging for a starter flock. By 1899, Oregon had sent pheasants to Washington, California, Arizona, New Mexico, Idaho, New Jersey, Massachusetts, Montana, Colorado, Oklahoma, Kansas, Arkansas, Missouri, Iowa, Illinois, Indiana, Ohio, Tennessee, Georgia, Virginia and Pennsylvania. Some states tried to get birds from China, too, but few arrived safely. Most birds shipped in small crates or baskets just couldn't stand the trip.

More letters went out to Oregon. Minnesota got its first pheasants from Oregon in 1905. The birds did well, but it would be nineteen years before there were enough to open the first hunting season. California had had pheasants from Oregon since 1889. But there was no hunting season until 1925, and then only in one small area. State-wide hunting in California didn't come until 1933.

Most of those who wrote to Oregon were state

A young hunter shows the results of his hunting trip in the 1920's.

Hunters should always respect the wishes of landowners.

game officers or the officers of private hunting clubs. But the first pheasants in Redfield, South Dakota, in 1908, were brought by Burt Hagman, a young man who had married a girl from Oregon. He wanted his bride to see the same beautiful birds in Redfield that she had known and loved at home.

Soon there were pheasants all over the state. In 1943, the ring-necked pheasant was named South Dakota's state bird. Now each December, when

drink from puddles or the raindrops caught in leaves or flower cups. But a nearby brook is better.

Water usually attracts insects. The pheasants may not know that this is a good reason for nesting near a stream. They go where they can feed on grasshoppers, beetles, flies, ants, crickets, cutworms and caterpillars. Spiders, earthworms, toads, mice, snails and small snakes are also favorite foods found near water.

Plants often grow best near water, too, and most of the pheasant's menu is plant food. These birds feast on blackberries, elderberries, hawthorn and sumac berries, apples, grapes and cherries. They nibble a few buds, but mostly eat the seeds of bristle grass, tarweed, thistle, chickweed, ragweed, dandelion, burdock, clover and sunflower. Of course, they also eat wheat, oats, corn, barley and buckwheat. Much of this is waste grain left behind by the harvesting machines.

The cock pheasant doesn't have all these foods in mind, but knows a good place when he sees one. A place with food, water and shelter just looks right to him.

On that first March morning he will call again and again, perhaps as often as every three or four minutes. After each call he will listen.

Can he hear an answering call near at hand? Is a rival cock out there trying to claim the same territory — or territory so near that the two will overlap?

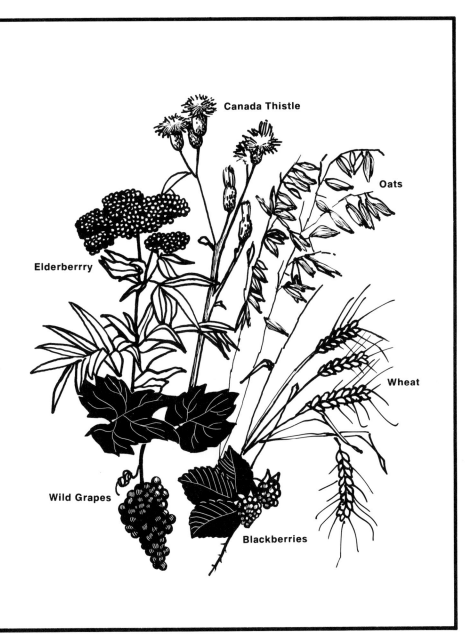

Some favorite pheasant foods.

If a rival cock should come strutting into view, there will likely be a fight. For a moment, the two rivals may just stand there — feathers raised, eyes flashing, tail plumes flared out behind. Then one cock takes a step forward and both leap to attack. For weapons they have strong wings to strike sharp blows, a sharp beak and, most dangerous of all, two spurs (the hind claw of each foot) always ready to slash and stab.

Only the cock has fighting spurs on its legs (left); cocks often soar high into the air when fighting over territory (right).

Most of the time a pheasant war dance is for show. One cock quickly realizes that the other is stronger. At the first chance, the weaker bird slinks away. Slinking is one of the things pheasants do very well. One moment the bird is there in plain sight. The next moment it is gone. It fades away into the tall grasses, leaving scarcely a ripple to mark the trail. The bird that slinks away will find a place somewhere else and hens of his own. He is not a loser.

If the only answering challenge comes from far away, the cock scarcely listens. After all, he isn't trying to claim all the land there is, just enough for need. He will claim no more than he can defend.

During the month of March the cock will crow again and again. He makes his claim first from one lookout post and then another until his boundaries are well marked. Every cock within a half-mile range will hear him and know what land is his. So will every listening hen. One or two hens, perhaps three or four, are nearby, waiting, and watching.

April — choosing a mate

April is courting time, the time for choosing mates. The cock takes the lead, stepping up boldly to his first choice. The others hens will have their turn, but he courts one at a time. He begins by showing-off, turning his head this way and that, so the hen has full view. Two dark feather tufts, one behind each ear, stand upright now. Dark neck feathers gleam, now blue, now green in changing light. Gold and bronze breast feathers shine. The red skin patches on his cheeks are brighter, puffier, more eye-catching than at any other season. Brown tail feathers are touched with pale rose. Beak to tail-tip he measures nearly a yard (92 cm) and every inch of it adds to his splendor.

The feather tufts are visible on the back of this cock's head.

A hen pheasant blends in with her surroundings.

The hen is only twenty-two to twenty-five inches (56-64 cm) instead of the cock's thirty to thirty-six (77-92 cm). Her tail is also shorter. It is only eleven or twelve inches (28-31 cm) instead of the cock's twenty to twenty-one (51-54 cm). From a distance she looks light and dark brown, but she has soft touches of lavender and rose, too.

Now the cock circles slowly around the hen. Suddenly he gives a little sideways dance step, lifting the wing facing her, ruffling out every feather so that he seems to double in size. He turns, circles again, strutting, stomping, bowing, showing off every bright feather. At last he gives a low clucking invitation to feed with him, to eat the food he has just found with quick searching eyes — some seeds, a tender bud, perhaps an insect or two. If she accepts, each knows that the choice is made.

They will mate. The cock and hen will also mate several times more during the next two weeks so that the hen can lay fertile eggs that will hatch into chicks.

The two will walk and feed together a part of each day. While the hen is with him she will eat the food he shows her. He clucks, pecking at the ground or scratching to mark the place where the food can be found. She comes right away. But when she is alone, the hen finds her own food just as easily.

Soon the cock chooses another mate, wooing her as she waits alone, using the same courting dance, the same invitation to eat. He will walk and feed with her, too, a part of each day. Perhaps he will choose a third mate, even a fourth. The number of mates is something neither cock nor hen needs to think about. This is just the way of the pheasant. If a hen feels that this cock has not found a good place to live, she may try to walk away. But usually the invitation is accepted.

April to May — choosing a nest

Each hen seeks out her own nesting place. The cock usually walks with her as she makes the search, but the choice is hers. When she finds a likely place, well hidden by tall grass or over-hanging branches, she will test it out. Does it feel as good as it looks?

The hen looks for good cover, like tall grasses, to hide her nest.

the first chick hatches in the early dawn-light and all ten or twelve will be out and about by mid-morning.

A chick has to break open its own shell. To make the first crack it taps the shell with a sharp knob on its beak called an egg tooth. After the chick has hatched, this will drop off. Once the crack is there,

This drawing shows the egg tooth on the tip of a chick's beak.

the chick turns, twists and squirms trying to get out of the sticky shell. Sometimes half of the shell will stick to the chick. For a minute or two it stumbles around looking like a ping-pong ball with legs and a head. But at last it is free. There it stands on wobbly pink legs, a bright-eyed ball of damp fluff.

The fluff, as it dries, shows colors of buffy yellow flecked with patches of brown. Those are nature's good camouflage colors. They copy the brown and yellow of sunlight as it shows through the leaves and branches overhead and falls on the ground. As long as the chick stands still, it will not be seen easily.

But standing still is not the way to learn about life. So the hen clucks to her brood of chicks, asking them to follow her. There is much for them to learn and only the few weeks of summer for lessons.

The first lesson is always on how to find food. Many baby birds, such as robins and sparrows, are hatched blind and helpless. They stay in the nest two or three weeks and the parents bring them food. All they have to do is open their mouth, swallow, and cry for more. But the baby pheasants and other chicken and duck-like birds are hatched ready to run, ready to find their own food. The hen only shows them where to look and what to choose.

The hen leads the chicks to a spot where caterpillars, ants, or other bugs can be found. She pecks at one or two herself to get them started. Most chicks don't need a second lesson. Hunger sets them to pecking at anything and everything until they find things they like. At first, smaller insects are their chief food. Like most baby birds, they must eat almost their own weight in food each day in order to grow to full size in one summer.

June to October — Growing time

For the first few days a baby pheasant doesn't do much growing. As long as it is covered with fluffy down it stays about the same size. When the feathers begin to grow, so does the chick. By the time it is eleven days old the main wing feathers are about two inches long. The little spike feathers of the tail are almost an inch. Most chicks now weigh about twice as much as they did on hatching day, about thirty grams or just over an ounce.

By the time the chicks are two weeks old, most of the back and side feathers are full length. At three or four weeks the breast, head and neck are feathered, too. By the time they are five weeks old, they have a full coat of brown baby feathers.

Before another week goes by, the chicks shed the baby feathers and begin to get a full adult coat. These feathers grow slowly. The breast feathers come first and by the seventh week you can tell a

young cock from his sisters by the gold and bronze-tone coloring. Now the young cock will try to copy his father's KOK! KOK! challenge. However, he still doesn't have the feathers to clap his wings. He is now beginning to grow the sharp spur on each leg that will one day be a ready weapon.

Around the eleventh week a young cock sheds his spike tail and begins to grow the long plumes. By the seventeenth or eighteenth week — mid September or early October — both hens and cocks of the year's hatch will have full adult feathers, though not yet full weight. Young cocks have all their breast feathers, but they will not shine with full golden gleam for another two months and spurs are not yet full length.

A young cock hides in the grass.

All through this growing time, the chicks have been learning the ways of the pheasant. They have learned from their parents' lessons and their own experiences.

If the chicks are caught where they cannot hide, or if an enemy comes too close, either cock or hen may take off in plain sight to draw attention away from the chicks. Or perhaps the hen will pretend to have a broken wing or a lame leg. She will hop and flutter, catching the eye of any hungry prowler. About the time that prowler is ready to leap, however, she will be off in a whir of wings. Meanwhile, the chicks have had time to slip under cover.

Sometimes an enemy comes too suddenly for these tricks to work. Then the cock takes instant flight with a loud alarm cry, a stuttering, ear-splitting **Ter-ut! Tut-tut! Tut-tut-t-t-t-tut-t-t-t!** Up he

A cock takes off with a loud alarm call!

springs with a rattling of wings to match the clattering cry. The prowler often stops in his tracks, too surprised to move. By the time the prowler comes to his senses, there's not a chick in sight. That is what usually happens. If the prowler is too wise to be fooled, then either cock or hen is ready to fight with wings, beak, and spurs.

November to February — winter comes

When winter comes with cold and snow or chilling rains, young pheasants may or may not stay where they were hatched. Young cocks are more likely to wander away than young hens. But both may stay, if there is enough food. Other young pheasants from a nearby place where food is scarce may also join them.

In winter, the cocks are not rivals. There is no courting or mating. Whether cock or hen, oldster or yearling, each thinks only of staying alive. In the winter, when hawks, owls and all four-footed meat-eaters are always hungry, it is easier to stay alive in a large flock than a small one. Older and wiser birds can help the others find food and shelter. Also, in a large flock there are enough birds to keep watch in every direction. Even the boldest raider cannot often sneak up for a surprise attack. Groups of thirty or forty, even more, may be seen in good pheasant country.

Like most wild animals, pheasants can go many days without food. They live on the fat stored in their bodies by over-eating in autumn. They often do not mind the cold. Their feathers lie in many layers and keep them warm in most winter weather.

Yet winter can bring hardship, and even death. Ice storms and freezing rain can all be deadly. The birds may smother beneath a snow drift. Ice may cling to face and beak so they cannot breathe. Most cocks live only two or three years, at best. Hens, not usually hunted, may live a year or so longer. Some pheasants have lived eight years, and with protection might live even longer. At times, only three or four pheasants, out of any ten birds that lived to summer's end, will be alive to start another spring.

Yet for a few, spring does come again. The cleverest and strongest cocks will claim the best nesting places, as they have always done. Young cocks will wander, looking for land and mates of their own. And the pheasant year from March to March will go around again.

CHAPTER THREE:

Pheasants and people – a shared world

Ring-necked pheasants, like most wild birds, do not make good pets. For one reason, they do not like to be caged. They may fight so hard to get free that they hurt themselves and die. Even if they accept the cage they may be in trouble. If everything they need — food, water and shelter — is just handed to them, they often lose all their wild instincts. They may become mean and bossy. Often they aren't smart enough to stay out of the way of a swinging door, let alone a cat or fox. They don't know how to get away from a speeding car, bicycle, or children at play.

Many people around the world raise pheasants as a hobby. They get together and have shows, and contests, and give prizes for the best birds. Most of these show birds are golden pheasants, silvers, or other fancy kinds, not ring-necks.

To learn about such groups in your area, ask your librarian for American Pheasant and Waterfowl Society Magazine.

Pheasants for hunters

Ring-necked pheasants are a favorite game bird for hunters all across the continent. Because many hunters want to go out after pheasants each autumn and winter, there aren't always enough birds to go around.

Game officers in each state have set hunting laws so both birds and hunters will have a fair chance and a challenge. Hunting can be done only during certain weeks, usually autumn and winter. Only a specific number of birds can be taken by any one hunter, and each hunter must buy a pheasant hunting license.

To meet the need for more pheasants, most states began to raise ring-necks on game-bird farms. As soon as a hen laid a few eggs, they would be taken from her nest and put into incubating machines. Then the hen would lay more eggs.

Farms can raise more chicks, but not smarter chicks. For many reasons, farm-raised chicks seem to lose all their wild instincts. They never have a chance to learn by watching their parents in the wild. Most of the yearling, farm-raised birds that are set free are killed by animals or hunters within a few weeks. They just don't know all the clever ways to stay alive that wild birds learn. These pheasants can't learn from their own experience until it is too late.

Most hunters and game officers agree that the best way to have more pheasants is to give wild birds more and better habitat. Better habitat means better food, water and shelter. Some of the money paid by pheasant hunters for a license is used by the state to buy land that will be good pheasant habitat. Groups of hunters and other interested persons have also raised money to buy land and plant it with grasses, berry patches and the kinds of trees and underbrush pheasants need for food and shelter. The sums spent by both the state and private groups can run into thousands and even millions of dollars. South Dakota is one of the states that leads in such action.

During the 1920's, South Dakota had over twenty million pheasants; because of a loss of habitat, their numbers fell to about one million by the 1970's. Thanks to smart game management they're now increasing again.

Like the Dennys, who paid for the first pheasants sent to Oregon over a century ago, people of South Dakota feel that having these beautiful birds is worth the price. Between 1977 and 1981, South Dakota hunters gave over $2.5 million for habitat restoration.

Farmers in South Dakota and other states also pledge their help. They may give money, but they also give or lend their land, promising to keep some area as good pheasant habitat. In Ohio, a number of farmers keep at least three acres for the pheasants out of every eighty acres owned.

A ring-neck pauses for a drink.

Many farmers have agreed to leave hedges and strips of wild grassland between fields, instead of plowing to the edge. Corners, gullies or steep slopes are allowed to grow up in a wild tangle that will provide pheasants with food and shelter. Here and there a small patch of clover will be fenced in and left for the pheasants. Roadside ditches are often left unmowed, so that they add even more good habitat.

Anyone who wants to help save wildlife can join farmers and hunters in these plans to give the pheasants better habitat.

All in all

Pheasants help farmers by eating hundreds of weed seeds that might otherwise grow up to crowd out crops. They eat hundreds of insect pests — including the gypsy moth, tent caterpillars and fruit flies that do heavy damage.

For the rest of us, there is pleasure enough just in watching the pheasants. Clucking hen and downy chicks, half-grown birds in follow-the-leader parade, the ring-necked cock springing up with rattling wings and a clattering cry. These birds share our world, and by sharing they challenge us to learn their ways.

**Almost all
ring-necked pheasants
in North America
are found within
the shaded areas**

WILDLIFE
HABITS & HABITAT

READ AND ENJOY THE SERIES:

THE **WHITETAIL** • THE **PHEASANT**

THE **BALD EAGLE** • THE **WOLVES**

THE **SQUIRRELS** • THE **BEAVER**

THE **GRIZZLY** • THE **MALLARD**

THE **RACCOON** • THE **WILD CATS**

THE **RATTLESNAKE** • THE **SHEEP**

THE **ALLIGATOR** • THE **CARIBOU**

THE **CANADA GOOSE** • THE **FOXES**

AAP-2153

OCT 18 1989